FORETASTE

FORETASTE

Poems
by
Peggy Pond Church

New Foreword
by
Peter Deckert

SOUTHWEST HERITAGE SERIES

SUNSTONE
PRESS

SANTA FE

Sunstone books may be purchased for educational, business, or sales promotional use.
For information please write: Special Markets Department, Sunstone Press,
P.O. Box 2321, Santa Fe, New Mexico 87504-2321.

Printed on acid-free paper
∞

Library of Congress Cataloging-in-Publication Data

Church, Peggy Pond, 1903-1986.
  [Poems. Selections]
  Foretaste : poems / by Peggy Pond Church.
    pages cm. -- (Southwest Heritage Series)
  "New Foreword by Peter Deckert."
  ISBN 978-0-86534-141-8 (softcover : alk. paper)
  I. Title.
  PS3505.H946F6 2014
  811'.52--dc23
                          2013045653

WWW.SUNSTONEPRESS.COM
SUNSTONE PRESS / POST OFFICE BOX 2321 / SANTA FE, NM 87504-2321 /USA
(505) 988-4418 / ORDERS ONLY (800) 243-5644 / FAX (505) 988-1025

CONTENTS

I

THE SOUTHWEST HERITAGE SERIES

"The past is not dead. In fact, it's not even past."
—William Faulkner, *Requiem for a Nun*

The history of the United States is written in hundreds of regional histories and literary works. Those letters, essays, memoirs, biographies and even collections of fiction are often first-hand accounts by people who wanted to memorialize an event, a person or simply record for posterity the concerns and issues of the times. Many of these accounts have been lost, destroyed or overlooked. Some are in private or public collections but deemed to be in too fragile condition to permit handling by contemporary readers and researchers.

However, now with the application of twenty-first century technology, nineteenth and twentieth century material can be reprinted and made accessible to the general public. These early writings are the DNA of our history and culture and are essential to understanding the present in terms of the past.

The Southwest Heritage Series is a form of literary preservation. Heritage by definition implies legacy and these early works are our legacy from those who have gone before us. To properly present and preserve that legacy, no changes in style or contents have been made. The material reprinted stands on its own as it first appeared. The point of view is that of the author and the era in which he or she lived. We would not expect photographs of people from the past to be re-imaged with modern clothes, hair styles and backgrounds. We should not, therefore, expect their ideas and personal philosophies to reflect our modern concepts.

Remember, reading their words and sharing their thoughts is a passport back into understanding how the past was shaped and how it influenced today's world.

Our hope is that new access to these older books will provide readers with a challenging and exciting experience.

PEGGY POND CHURCH

II

FOREWORD
to
This Edition
by
Peter Dechert

We found life is not what we dream but something that dreams us.
—Peggy Pond Church, "Letter to Virginia"

Some poets create transparent poems. Others create opaque poems.

By this, I mean that one can see through transparent poems to the poets themselves, but one catches few glimpses of the poets behind opaque poems. Opaque poems are not necessarily hard to understand: if you have a year or so to spare for the task, read through Longfellow's collected works. You'll understand just about all of them, but you'll also come away with very little perception of just what sort of a real person Longfellow was. His poetry is opaque simply because he did not put much of himself into what he wrote.

Another variety of opaque poems is those whose actual meaning seems to be unclear, for example Ezra Pound's "Cantos." In these cases, we seem to see the poet struggling to express ideas that he himself had not yet fully apprehended: the reader may decide that the poet had bitten off more than he could chew, could not digest it, could not fully transmit himself or his ideas to the reader because he was unsure just who "himself" or what "his ideas" might be.

Peggy Pond Church was active during a time frame within which hindsight suggests the latter sort of opacity seemed to predominate. Scholars were citing works by Pound, T. S. Eliot, Wallace Stevens, William Carlos Williams, and others like them as being models of "avant-garde" poetic construction. Most critics seemed to think during the middle years of the twentieth century that poets had to tackle difficult, obscure subjects aggressively in order to be worthy of serious consideration, even if they never reached satisfactory resolutions.

Robert Frost probably came closer than any of Peggy's contemporaries to breaking this trend in scholarly judgment. He occupied a sort of middle ground: on the scale I have suggested, we might call Frost a translucent poet. He was essentially objective: we could understand his poems, but not always be quite sure where he himself stood in relation to a number of them. Were they simply observations, or did they reflect firmly held convictions, basic beliefs?

Peggy made transparent poems.

Reading Peggy's poems today, we realize that we are immediately, even intimately, in touch with Peggy herself. In a very real sense, Peggy's poems were, and still are, Peggy. We discover Peggy through them. They were created out of her convictions, convictions that she was able to translate into meaningful words, phrases, sentences: entities. Created, too, out of her emotions. She had no hesitation when it came to tackling difficult subjects, nor any fear of facing her subject matter head-on. And once she had made her poem, no reader could doubt that he had been spoken to by a real person, wholly involved.

My acquaintance with Peggy went through two phases, with an interval of almost thirty years. The first phase was during my two years at the Los Alamos Ranch School, from which I graduated in 1941. Fermor Church, Peggy's husband, known universally to his friends as "Ferm," was our Assistant Headmaster and principal science teacher. Peggy, it seems to me, was our principal iconoclast.

Peggy's father, Ashley Pond Jr., started a guest ranch on the Pajarito Plateau about 1912; in 1917 he founded what was at first a sort of recuperative facility, largely for boys from the east who had become ill; this facility had developed into the Ranch School twenty-two years before I arrived in 1939. Thus, as a youngster, Peggy spent formative years in the mesa and mountain country on the Plateau; she quickly grew to love it. And she explored it thoroughly both then and later, on horseback, on foot, climbing—and no doubt sometimes falling.

Pond, a concept person, not an educator, employed A. J. Connell to be the School's "Director" almost immediately after it was established. Connell, born in New York City, came to Pond's attention when he was reassigned to Santa Fe in 1914, after having been in the Forest Service in Silver City, New Mexico; he was an enthusiastic Boy Scout leader as well as a Forest Ranger in both locations. Like Pond, Connell had had no experience as an academic educator, and in fact had never been to college. His goal in the beginning was to train the boys to be at the same time obedient and independent: ultimately self-sufficient within any set of circumstances. This goal was totally in accord with Pond's own concept for the school. Pond left the Ranch School in Connell's hands in 1917 in order to try to become an army pilot in San Diego. When he returned to New Mexico, it was to live in Santa Fe, not at Los Alamos.

In 1918, after the School's first year, "AJ" (a universally applied nickname, though he was also called by students "The Boss" behind his back) hired Fayette Curtis to oversee the formal education process, and devoted himself to training his boys to handle their lives within this environment. He retained final control, however, over everything that happened on the Ranch.

Ferm Church arrived at the School from Harvard a few years later. He and Peggy fell in love and were married in 1924, after she had spent two years at Smith College. AJ had many prejudices, among which was a disapproval of employing married teachers to live at the School with their wives. But Peggy was Ashley Pond's daughter, and AJ had to make the best of it and put up with the situation. Peggy, as independent a soul as ever was, insisted on going her own way instead of bowing to AJ's expectations for the behavior of a Master's wife; the result was mutual antipathy that only increased with the years that followed. I recall sitting in classes some mornings and, on looking out the window, seeing Peggy riding into distances all her own, galloping the hum-drum of the School away in search of her personal freedom. Then, I envied her.

By the later 1930s, ten years after L. S. Hitchcock became Headmaster following Curtis's death, the School had been further revamped, with increased emphasis on the academic area. By then, too, it had become the custom at dinner for Masters to preside over most of the tables for six at which we ate in the Fuller Lodge, and if a Master was married (as happened increasingly in later years, AJ's prejudice notwithstanding) his wife was supposed to sit at the foot of his table. Peggy avoided this task at every opportunity. She did, after all, have three sons to raise; but by the time I came to Los Alamos they were old enough to take care of themselves. Two, indeed, were enrolled as students. No matter, it is a fact that we saw less of Peggy than of any other wife, though she did seem to enjoy helping to coach us in the annual Gilbert and Sullivan operettas that we learned to perform.

It remains a wonder to me that my copy of *Foretaste* was inscribed to me personally by Peggy on the day of my graduation. I have it still, of course.

Almost three decades later my wife and I and our three daughters moved permanently here to Santa Fe. Following several years in Taos, where in 1944 Fermor had tried unsuccessfully to reestablish the Ranch School a year and a half after the government had commandeered the area that was centered on the original school site, he and Peggy moved to Berkeley; but by the time my family and I arrived they had moved back to live in Santa Fe. I looked them up. Though they were a generation older than we, we formed a comfortable friendship, visiting each other for meals and talking about the almost always astounding current developments that surface in Santa Fe. After Ferm died in 1975, we still visited with Peggy from time to time, until our own several involvements in Santa Fe's community concerns began to take center stage in our lives, while Peggy herself seemed to grow even more intensely private than she had used to be. She was, although we did not realize it then, working at putting together her final volumes of poetry.

In all our conversations, I do not remember ever having discussed poetry with Peggy: hers or anyone else's. In 1969 I was asked to become the "Founding President" of the New Mexico Poetry Society through a series of laughable errors. I also resumed making some poems of my own. But I cannot recall having even mentioned this fact to her. I guess I instinctively realized that Peggy was concerned with doing poetry, not talking poetry.

Now, a special problem intervenes when it comes to reading "transparent" poems: if the poet is engaged with the topic of her poem to the point of being preoccupied with it, the result may be a number of poems on the same theme, expressing essentially identical points of view. It is hard to read a group of them consecutively without being numbed by the experience. Thus, for example, almost all but the final few poems in Peggy's *Ultimatum for Man* become a real struggle for the reader who elects to take them at a single sitting. She felt passionately about the ruinous effects of World War II on boys-become-soldiers; passionately about the advent of atomic war, about what she saw as the probable demise of civilization and the entire apparently bleak future for mankind—including, far from least, her own sons. Any one or two of these poems taken by itself is impressive, but the totality of all of them experienced at once leaves the reader with a somewhat bitter taste of overkill.

Something like this is also true with the poems that she published about her marriage. She and Ferm were as different as two folk in love could possibly be. Ferm was the practical, down-to-earth scientist and technician personified, concerned with the here, the now, the facts of whatever matter he was investigating. Peggy was the dreamer, in a sense the philosopher, concerned with the myriad possible outcomes rather than the dollars-and-cents sort of single resolution that Ferm had been trained to seek. In a poem celebrating their fortieth wedding anniversary, Peggy expressed their dilemma in these words:

"I like exploring things.
You like knowing what they are made of."

These very different outlooks appear on reading Peggy's poems to have led to some bleak interludes in their long life together, first explored by Peggy in Part I of *Familiar Journey* (1936). The poetic sequence here begins with happiness, travels through turmoil and travail, suggests a short-lived resolution, and ends with something approaching despair, reflecting the actual events of her personal life and hospitalization. But if there was one thing Peggy knew, it was that no matter the differences in their perceptions, she could always count on Ferm to be there for her in his own way.

This never-quite-resolved difference in outlooks forms the entire corpus of *The Ripened Fields: Fifteen Sonnets of a Marriage*, published following Ferm's death forty years after *Familiar Journey* appeared. The final sonnet, indeed, was written for Ferm posthumously; but the other fourteen, quite different in style from the one that ends the collection, are said to have been written much earlier, between 1943 and 1953. As a matter of fact, Part I of *Familiar Journey* incorporates seven sonnets (including the dedicatory one) written in the very same tone and style found in the first fourteen sonnets of *The Ripened Fields*. Since *Familiar Journey* was released in 1936, I believe that all these sonnets, as well as other poems in the same vein, suggest that it took a long while before resolution finally came as the result of having shared and finally melded two lifetimes of outlook and experience.

What is worthy of note in all this, however, is that Peggy never blamed Ferm for being who he was: she blamed herself for not being able to be someone who she wasn't. And all I can add is that, when we renewed our acquaintance in 1969, I saw no signs of any sort of stress between Peggy and Ferm. They were happy together.

Their personal history does not really matter now, nor to us. The only reason I have brought it up is to show a second instance in which, if you read all the pertinent poems at one or two sittings, their totality may become overwhelming: Peggy may perhaps have sometimes created too many variations on a single theme. Poets who hold passionate convictions often do so.

Many of us, as we travel, come upon a scene that particularly attracts us. If we are carrying a camera we may photograph what we see so that we will be able to recall it in years to come. We make its image. Peggy also saw the landscape about her as she walked, rode, and drove through New Mexico's mountains, mesas, and canyons. But she was gifted with a very special ability to add her imagination to the simple image. She saw her surroundings not only as they existed at the moment, but as they might exist in other moments, under different conditions of weather, with other birds in the trees, or with the older cliff-dwelling people still active around them. These special insights illuminate her poems: Peggy seeing things in ways that more mundane folk are not fitted to recognize or record.

No sensitive reader should ever sit down to read a volume of poetry all at once, not even volumes as short as Peggy's are. Each poem worth its salt should be considered and reconsidered before one moves on to the next one, and three or four at one sitting is really a temporary surfeit. Do not sit down to browse through a book of Peggy's poems, short as it may seem: what you hold in your hand is an important fraction of the labor of seventy-odd years.

Truly, Peggy did see not only the things that the rest of us see, but saw them as they may once have been and as they may someday be. All at once. She often saw totality. The poems in the second part of *Familiar Journey* are superb, to choose just one set of examples from amongst them all. And through these transparent poems, we see Peggy herself, a lyric poet of subtle nobility. Her work deserves our notice: everyone's notice.

III

REVIEW

The New Mexico Quarterly, February, 1934, Volume IV, Number 1

Foretaste—Peggy Pond Church—Writers' Editions,
Santa Fe—$2.00.

I opened Peggy Pond Church's volume of verse, *Foretaste*, and was aware of light fingers picking up earth and fashioning it into winged thoughts. Here are pages with delicately-carved poems, fragrant with the sage of high mesas, light as a cirrus cloud, warm as red blood, vibrant as the strings of a violin. The reader catches glimpses, feels touches of the sensitive character of the poet, sensitive not so much to darkness as to light in all its nuances of color, movement, and design. Of acid there is not a trace. There are cloud-shadows, the flight of a fairy, altars, the turn of the earth, lilac roots, turquoise in the wind.

The author has divided her book into two parts, but the poems arrange themselves into four spheres: poems close to the earth, fantasy, sketches of children, glimpses of the native Southwest. New Mexico is symbolized in a new way: placid burros become ancient hills; chili burns with new fever; natives pray in the cool recesses of a church under an anciently carved statue of Joseph; sheep and goats whiten the rock-ribbed hills. You will enjoy "Sheep Country" and "A Miracle of Santuario" and the mystery of "Abiquiu" and walk the petalled streets of Rosario in "Admonition."

If the reader inclines toward modern poetry, he will like the way Mrs. Church brings out new thoughts and expresses them in new ways. This is brought out in "Changeling," the story of a fay who "lay like a wind against a man's shoulder" and "danced like a crisp gold leaf." In a fantastic way Mrs. Church talks about peach orchards in early spring and the mystery of a shadow made by a saffron bough in "Shadow-Madness." Rain, "a scud of color down a roadway" clears poetic thought to a filigree mist. "The sky was a crystal bell that was cupped upon me" brings an intangible something into incandescent lines. With a delicate touch she brings atmosphere into "For an Autumn Moment," which first appeared in the *New Mexico Quarterly*, and "Open Winter." Love of sheer lyricism is increased after reading the sonnets "Evergreen," "Bridal," and "Bondage." An original characteristic of her work is the use of kennings which she has revived from the old English. Slant-winged, grass-hidden, winter-driven, earth-colored, sky-color—she fills her poems with intimate glimpses such as these—words which give a definite flavor and a freshness to her poetry. Mrs. Church writes poems that are close to the earth, which have themes ringing through them with the tone of Millay. The desire "to go back to the earth, give birth to mountains, be intimate with the tide and the rain and the seasons" is the theme of the poems "Foretaste," "I Have Looked at the Earth," "Ceremonial," and "To Certain Ones Who Do Not Understand." There is pathos giving way to thanksgiving in the starkly simple "Drought" where rain-clouds disappear "across the hard laughter of the sky."

Perhaps her rhyming verse is better than her free verse, and it is difficult to accustom the silent ear where rhyming gives way to a rugged splattering of words as in "A Miracle of Santuario." But there will be light in the heart after reading "Five Years Old" and "A Dower for My Daughter," and there will be always tousled brown curls and a mouth as bright and as gay as a barberry after "Not Quite Three," and there will be the pang that goes with a star in "For a Birthnight" and the homey charm of "Song for Hanging Out Clothes."

If, gentle reader, you go around and around in the dull brown days of life and never see a lark burst into stars, read Peggy Pond Church's *Foretaste*.

—Harvena Conrad Richter

IV

OBITUARIES

Santa Fe Style, November 19, 1986
Peggy Pond Church
by
Geoff Gorman

In 1942 Peggy Pond Church found herself at the center of two worlds changing: The Old West outpost of Los Alamos where she had grown up was suddenly taken over by the United States government for the Manhattan Project to develop the atomic bomb. Her coming down from the mesas and canyons of the formerly unknown village on Pajarito Plateau was a journey that took the rest of her life.

For most of the years of her life, Church was a writer. And in her prose and poetry she explored the once-sacred world of the Indians on her familiar mesas and the encroachment by the government, which was to produce there the most powerful instrument of destruction that the world had ever known. Hers was a voice of outrage at one time, but later, through her poetry, she came to be reconciled to what fate had chosen for her beloved land.

Church died on Thursday, Oct. 23, apparently by suicide, at her apartment in a retirement complex in Santa Fe. Some persons close to her said that she had become increasingly despondent over the infirmities of old age, and ended her life by taking a lethal dose of drugs. She was 82 years old.

Her first poem was written when she was only a child, and her last book of poetry, "Birds of Daybreak: Landscapes and Elegies," was published just last year. But Church is perhaps most widely known for her book "The House at Otowi Bridge," published in 1960, in which through recollections of her former neighbor Edith Warner she contrasts the land that she loved as a young girl with the changes brought to Los Alamos by the coming of the nuclear scientists in the early 1940s.

She was born on Dec. 1, 1903, near Watrous, N.M., to Ashley Pond Jr.

and Hazel Hallett Pond. She had a younger brother who died several years ago and a sister who lives in Oregon.

Most of her childhood was spent on Pajarito Plateau where her father built the Los Alamos Ranch School in 1917. Growing up in the Jemez Mountains, the youngster often roamed the nearby mesas and canyons on horseback, learning to appreciate the wilderness setting.

By the age of 11 she had written her first poem, and while she was in high school one of her short stories won $50 in a student competition offered by the Atlantic Monthly.

At an early age she was known for her wonderful sense of humor, recalled her sister, Dorothy Benedict. "She would tell people we were heiresses to Ponds Cold Cream," Benedict said with a laugh. "But we weren't really related."

She attended several boarding schools in the East and the West, and spent two years studying at Smith College in Massachusetts. In 1924 she left college to marry H. Fermor Spencer Church, who was a faculty member at her father's school.

In her early married years she was the only faculty wife at the school. Her father had retired to live in Santa Fe, and had hired a man named A.J. Connell to run the school. An avid rider and lover of mountain trails, Church was often in disagreement with Connell as to the proper behavior of a young faculty wife. And he often made his disapproval of her actions clear to her, according to her son Hugh Church. But his criticism was not enough to make her change her ways.

In the years leading up to the Second World War, Church was not only a mother and a wife, but also a successful writer who required her own privacy to do her work, her son said. "At the ranch she had a cabin on the edge of a canyon that she retreated to, to do her work," he recalled.

Her first book of poetry, "Foretaste," was published in 1933 by the Rydal Press in Santa Fe. "Familiar Journey," her second book of poems, followed in 1936, also published by Rydal Press.

"She was always torn between the practical things and the poet in her—always struggling between those two things," recalled Corina Santistevan, who had been her friend since 1946. "She lived many lives and related to many things. She was always curious, like a child. Every stone she had to feel, to touch, to pick up and weigh."

Although Los Alamos was a small town, it saw more and more visitors as the 1940s approach[ed]. One sojourner, Edith Warner, eventually became a permanent resident. She lived several miles south of town alongside the Rio Grande, in the small house that served as a train station and later as a teahouse serving many of the scientists and their families during the war years. It was eventually depicted in Church's book.

"It was Edith Warner in her little house by the bridge on the road to Los Alamos who saw it all happen," Church wrote, referring to the changes brought by the government scientists, in "The House at Otowi Bridge," which has become a Southwestern classic.

These changes were visited suddenly on the remote village of fewer than 200 inhabitants. In December 1942, a year after the United States entered World War II, Church and her family were informed that the school and their home were being taken over by the government in order to carry out a highly secret wartime project. Only 2 ½ years later, the Manhattan Project, under the direction of J. Robert Oppenheimer, would succeed with the world's first nuclear explosion at Trinity, a site in southern New Mexico. Weeks later atomic bombs would be dropped on Hiroshima and Nagasaki in Japan.

At the time, because her husband was a physics teacher Church suspected the nature of the scientific work being carried out by the government. But for her, immediately, it was an expulsion from paradise. And it forced her and her family to move to Taos, then to California, and finally again to Taos, where her husband tried unsuccessfully to open a school much like the one abandoned in Los Alamos. In 1960 the family settled in Santa Fe.

The knowledge of what Los Alamos had turned into haunted Church for the rest of her life, her sister commented. Church first expressed her outrage at the bomb in "Ultimatum for Man," a book of poetry published in 1946. However, as the years passed her outlook mellowed. After writing "The House at Otowi Bridge," she turned to writing about life, love and fate, often expressing her themes by drawing images from nature.

Throughout her life Church was constantly exploring the world, and she chose friends who were diverse in age, profession and race, recalled Santistevan. "They reflected her life," she commented.

Church had a great love for the ancestral home of the Indians in the Jemez Mountains, and had an abiding interest in all Native Americans and their lore. She particularly loved the mythical Indian character, Coyote, who could be blamed for any mishaps. "He's a trickster. He makes me lose things, forget," she said in an interview several years ago.

"Last Tuesday [before her death] when we spoke, I had a coyote story I thought Peggy might be interested in," Santistevan said. "She wanted to know who wrote it. I said that a New Yorker had written it, and we both laughed."

"She was a religious person in the universal sense," added Santistevan.

Church's husband died in 1975. A year later she published "New and Selected Poems," and in 1978 she published "The Ripened Fields: Fifteen Sonnets of a Marriage." In 1981 she published "A Rustle of Angels."

In 1984 she received a Governor's Award for her contributions to art. And a year later she published her last book of poetry, "Birds of Daybreak: Landscapes and Elegies."

For many years Church lived in a house on Camino Ranchitos, and about a year ago she moved into an apartment in the El Castillo Retirement Residences.

As she grew older Church developed a fondness for collecting native plants and rocks for her garden, remembered her friend and neighbor Mary Miam. Several days before Church's death, Miam brought her one of the rocks she treasured the most from the garden of her former home. "Her poetry reminded me of the rocks and flowers in her garden: delicate yet strong," Miam said.

Over the last several years Church developed allergies to many things in her environment, according to her son Hugh. She was also upset and frustrated at slowly losing her senses of sight and hearing. "She was so dependent upon her senses," remarked her son.

She was a "card-carrying" member of the Hemlock Society, which counsels people with terminal illnesses about suicide, her son Hugh said. Church often talked about how to deal with people as they got old and infirm, according to her son. "She put herself to sleep," he said, referring to her death.

She is survived by three sons, Theodore Church, Allen Church and Hugh Church, all of Albuquerque; a sister, Dorothy Benedict of Oregon; five grandchildren and three great-grand children.

The New Mexican, Sunday, October 26, 1986
by
The New Mexican Staff

Margaret "Peggy" Pond Church, a poet and author whose works recalled early days in northern New Mexico, died Thursday at home. She was 82.

Her father, Ashley Pond II, founded the Los Alamos Ranch School in 1916. The school became the site of the Manhattan Project, where the first atomic weapons were made.

Church's poems and books recalled growing up on Pajarito Plateau, a volcanic ash formation that includes the Los Alamos mesa, which became known as "The Hill."

In a 1981 interview with *The New Mexican*, she said she spent a lot of time outdoors and became an ardent lover of nature.

In *A Lament on Tsankawi Mesa*, she wrote about the changes that her much-loved hill had undergone:

> What has changed?
> Is it I who have changed?
> The light-footed child I was no longer answers
> the exuberant life has dwindled…
> Giant machines with an evil eye
> spread themselves over the mesa;…

Pond's *House at Otowi Bridge* told the Los Alamos story through the life of one woman, Edith Warner, who was a station master for the Denver and Rio Grande narrow-guage train. Her last book, *Birds of Daybreak*, was a collection of poetry printed in 1985.

Church was born in Watrous Dec. 1, 1903 to the late Ashley and Hazel Hallett Pond. Her husband of 50 years, Fermor S. Church, and her brother, Dr. Ashley Pond III, both died earlier.

She is survived by three sons, Theodore, Allen and Hugh, all of Albuquerque; six grandchildren; three great-grandchildren; and her sister, Dorothy Benedict of Glendale, Oregon.

A memorial service will be held by the Santa Fe Friends Meeting. The McGee Memorial is handling funeral arrangements.

Memorial donations may be made to The School of American Research in Santa Fe, St. John's College, or the Los Alamos Historical Society's Peggy Pond Church Endowment Fund.

V

EDITION OF 1933

FORETASTE

FORETASTE

PEGGY POND CHURCH

WRITERS' EDITIONS

Santa Fe, N. M.

Acknowledgment is made to the following magazines for permission
to reprint a number of these poems: To the *Atlantic Monthly* for
Foretaste, Shadow-madness, and To Certain Ones; to *The Pa-
rents' Magazine* for A Dower for my Daughter, If I Had a Young
Son, and Five Years Old; to *Poetry* for Drought, Song for Hanging
Out Clothes, and Escape; to the *New Mexico Quarterly* for For
an Autumn Moment; to the *Ladies' Home Journal* for Evergreen;
to *Scribners' Magazine* for Bondage; and to the editor of *Folk-
Say* for Sheep Country, A Miracle of Santuario, and Abiquiu.

This sight once, being beautiful, wrenched at my heart:
Birds flying west at the first edge of night.
They seemed to fly always above shadow and
            on the bright
Slanting last waves of sun, birds flying and singing.

And I had forgotten this till the other day
I was returning home by airplane and the clouds
            dripped sunlight
Flame-colored about us, and below us the twilight
Deepened and purpled the peach-trees,

And I thought: Now I too have known it;
That ecstasy of the birds, that last moment of flight
At the cloud's edge in a world above shadow,
            in a world beneath light.
I know why they flew, and why as they flew
            they were singing.

CONTENTS

I

FORETASTE

The day stood up around me, blue,
Farther than sight, and then I knew
The river was a blue track curled
Through the pale center of my world.
The mountains leaned against the sky,
Blue piled on blue, immensely high,
And in the sky a slant-winged bird
Moved slowly, like a singing word.
Onward I drove and saw the road
Unwind blue miles; the river flowed
Implacable and strong and wide,
Lifting pale waves, a hurrying tide,
And trees grew up along its brim
And higher towered the mesa's rim,
Drawing a black, unbroken line
Across blue sky as clear as wine,
So clear I almost saw a star,
Bright as infinity, and far.

I was not body-bound this day.
The mountains pulled me clear away.
Upward I burned like their blue flame;
Then turned my eyes and quickly came

In one short flight to colored hills
Where no leaf grows. The black rain spills
Out of fierce clouds on silver days
And carves steep earth in curious ways.
And then I lay, a sage-swept plain,
Slanting to riverward again.

I held low houses on my breast
And wide church doors that opened west.
With simple folk I knelt and prayed,
And in their bodies long I stayed.
With their own hands I shaped warm earth
To bricks, and in swept rooms gave birth
To many a child, and saw some die.
I felt my breasts grow old and dry.
My tear-spent eyes were deep and wise
And sorrowless as star-edged skies.
At last I died and became earth
Close to the house that saw my birth.

And suddenly this curious thing:
Like spinning earth I seemed to sing.
A spinning earth I then became
And whirled through space like a clear flame.
Mountains were part of me, and then
Made of the same flame I knew men.
Oh then I saw what death might be,
What keen, unfettered ecstasy
To be the earth, not just to see
Blue light spilled over hill and tree;

To feel the rain tread on my heart,
Not watch it shine, a thing apart;
And in all men to be the fire
Of grief and joy and swift desire.

My car moved slow. I felt the road
Weigh down upon me like a load.
I saw a woman brown of face
Hoeing hard earth with strong, sure grace.
I looked at her as at my friend.
I saw her turn from me and bend
Over her work. She did not know
I'd worn her flesh a while ago.
She did not even hear my cry.
Prisoned in body now was I.
I looked out on the gathering stars
As though my eyes were prison bars.

SHEEP COUNTRY

In spring the sheep are driven over the mountain
While there is still snow knee-deep in every shadow
And the wind's edge is sharp in the Valle country.
The sheep come up from the canyons
Like a grey cloud. They move slowly. They leave
          unnibbled
Not a low-growing leaf, not a sliver of grass,
Not a flower.

In Capulin canyon the river crossings are muddied
Before the wild choke cherries are in flower;
There are a hundred twisted trails on Rabbit mountain
Made by the sheep that come up from Peña Blanca,
From Cienega and Cochiti, from Santo Domingo,
From the dirty corrals, from the flat, dusty mesas
Where they have fed all winter.

I have seen them going up Santa Clara canyon in April
When Tsacoma mountain is still a white cloud of
          brightness
Lifted against the sky; when the wind is bitter
And there is only a haze of green around the aspens
You can see by looking slantwise, never directly,
Never in a second glance, never by coming closer.

I have seen the sheep move up Santa Clara canyon
And over the ridge
And down the Rito de los Indios and onward into
The long, curved Valle San Antonio.

And I have seen the names of the sheepherders written
On the aspen trees halfway up Tsacoma
And on Redondo mountain where the aspens fight
               for their rootholds
In the black rocks, in the frozen lava.
Casimiro Chaves, I have seen written; Juan Pino;
               Reyes Contreras;
From Chamita and Abiquiu and Española,
Nambé and Pojuaque.

These are the names of boys, carved here and written,
Whose wits, they say, aren't fit for any other work,
Or men whose minds are still the minds of children;
Who do not desire anything more of living
Than to lie in the glittering shadow of an aspen
On the rim of the Valles where the sheep feed
And move downward slowly.

There are men who desire much more and find much less.
Must we all be madmen, I wonder, or innocents
To follow the sheep along the ridge of the Valles,
Looking down, west, to the sea of grasses,
The far-off tangled, grass-hidden threads of water,
And the nets of rain through which the farther mountains
Shine like a shadow?

FOR AN AUTUMN MOMENT

Pause, like the earth, and shoulder the light of evening;
The light, and the light reflected in yellow water
Where the river turns and flows south against the mesa,
Thrusting the black rocks asunder with its singing
That never is hushed an instant, even at sundown,
When the world pauses, and you and I, and the leaves
         that hang windless
In the moment of changing to gold from the green
        of summer.

NOVEMBER

Out of a clear sky,
Out of a sky too clear for our believing,
So cloudless the very clouds are almost forgotten,
Comes now a black sea; wave upon wave of blackness
Winter-driven out of what chaos we know not,
Snow-frothed, white-tipped as the very waves of the ocean;
And the earth waits, like the shuddering rocks of
        the sea-cliffs,
For this wave of winter to break upon and submerge her.

OPEN WINTER

Spring will come
After a while to these tired, these snow-starved hills;
These hills that have known no rest the whole long
                    winter;
These hills that have lain
Under the pale, under the comfortless sky
Like a sleeper whom sleep has cheated.
Spring will come
Like a too early, a too persistent daylight
After the long, unrestful night and sleepless.
The trees will wearily once more put on their leaves,
The grass lift slightly.
The tired flowers will blossom one by one.
But the whole summer will be only a heavy-lidded
Waiting for autumn,
For a second winter,
Not like this one, never again like this one;
A winter of deep snow, of snow-heaped branches,
Of snow so deep along the ground not the earliest violet
But will sleep dreamlessly nor wake till April.

CRYSTAL

I lay, stretched out, flat on the sands of this river.
The sky was a crystal bell that was cupped upon me
In which no motion was nor any breathing.
It was as if the sky came down with the hills behind it,
And I saw the hills outside with their crying color,
Hyacinth and maize and pale jade, turquoise and lapis,
Outside the windless bell the sky made over me
Empty of all color but the color reflected beyond it,
So blue I looked on the hills as if through water.
They shimmered and melted and left me. They were
            forgotten.
I was only a shape, something in the small shape
            of a mountain;
The only mountain in this faintly curved earth that
            stretched forever
Like the curved thin shadows on the curve of a
            blown bubble.
In a moment my weight would burst it, my breath
            would break it
Unless I lay still and ceased from breathing forever.

ALIEN

I can never be one of them.
The forest will be friendly for a day;
The trees for a little while will be familiar
Suffering me to walk among them,
And I can lean on a rock and watch the water
Eating a way through harsh earth to its ocean.

But the trail bends.
The leaves turn dark in a shadow
And I remember that earth here once in anger
Spewed burning rock out of that close-glimpsed mountain
And that there is no one here who speaks my language,
Not tree, nor stone, nor time-oblivious river.

WHAT WILL THEY REMEMBER?

What will they remember
When winter closes their doorway
And heaps white snow against the window?
What will they remember
Back among sky-hiding buildings,
Back under sky-veiling clouds?

A black mesa watching
Above an earth-colored village;
Autumn-yellow leaves against a black mesa;
An Indian woman suckling a child near a house-wall;
Blue and yellow corn heaped in the doorway;
And always like a shadow
The black mesa pushing
Against the eye-blinding sky.

WINTER SKETCH

Today there is snow all over the valley,
And we ride in a little world hidden from
        the mountains.
The hills behind Pojuaque that are usually
        painted on the sky
The color of fire against the color of mountains,
Tonight are hyacinth pink on a grey cloud curtain,
Fading to violet, fading to no color at all.
And there is a house with a blue door and a
        blue-framed window
Like a reminder of the sky, and a lamp lit in it;
And three pigs; and a cow chewing her cud
        in a dooryard.
Finally only the noiseless, invisible snow pricking
        down out of darkness.

DROUGHT

She looked out at her door,
She looked out on the plain,
And all she saw was brown earth
Crying for rain.

She looked at the mountains,
She looked at the sky
And all she saw was shadows
Brittle and dry.

All she saw was shadows
Where no clouds were,
And an image of water
No wind could stir.

She saw the hot leaves hanging
Limp and wind-driven
On the apple-tree seedlings
Her mother had given.

And she watched a man bending
And straightening and stooping
Out in the field
Where the corn was drooping.

A dark bird circled
In the hot sky
And she knew some carrion
Rotted near-by,

She pressed tight fingers
Against her head.
It will drive me mad
Before long, she said.

She walked to the well
And suddenly cried
For the little peach tree
Had withered and died,

The little peach tree
That in the spring
Had shone and sung
At its blossoming.

This land is not barren—
She caught her breath—
It bears, but it bears
With the midwife, death!

She heard the wind
And her thoughts were wild
For ever since spring
She had carried a child.

And she feared the wind
That rasped in the corn
Lest it enter the house
Where her child was born.

Out where the fields lay aching in the sun
The man leaned on his hoe a moment and
                     watched the sky.
The rain will come, he said. It always comes.
Needs only to wait and know that it will come.
The rain will come, a tall god, like a lover
To the waiting earth.
Rain will come to the earth as a lover to his beloved,
Over the mountains darkly, over the sky.
He cannot rest from her forever;
He will hear her calling, he will come swiftly, surely,
Over the mountains.
He will lie like a dark cloud
In the arms of his beloved.

She watched from the doorway
His endless hoeing
Nor saw on the mountains
The small cloud growing.

She had seen clouds, she said,
Before,
And they always went sailing
Past her door.

They always went sailing
White and dry
Across the hard laughter
Of the sky.

She never could watch
A cloud again
With hope in her heart
And a smell of rain.

A light like glittering metal fell on the fields,
A light that was harsh and brittle, the color of brass.
The wind died out and left an empty space
Between heaven and earth. The climbing bird
Dropped into the void and disappeared.

She ran into the house
She closed the door,
She said she wouldn't be
Fooled any more.

She pulled the shades close
For her heart's sake.
when this storm passed over
Her heart would break.

The trees suddenly lifted up their wilted leaves;
The air turned silver;
The sky burned fiercely along the black edge
               of a cloud;
The wings of rain spread wide against the sky.

The man, bending with his hoe toward the earth
Felt the earth tremble, tremble as one who hears
The footsteps of her beloved on the mountain.

       The rain came down
       With a silver sound;
       The rain fell sweet
       On the thirsty ground.

       It whispered and sang
       On the upturned leaves;
       It rang like a cry
       From the dusty eaves.

       She heard it rushing,
       She heard it roar,
       She heard it beating
       Against the door.

       She heard in the cornfield
       The crisp leaves sing,
       And she ran out
       Like a mad, wild thing.

She loosened her hair,
She loosened her dress,
She lifted her arms
To the rain's caress.

It touched her eyes
That were dry and aching;
It touched her heart
That was burned and breaking.

Her gaze sought wide
And her gaze sought high,
She saw the cloud leaning
From the sky.

And she saw the man
Was bending again
To hoe a path
For the running rain.

Under her heart
She felt the child
Stir into life.
She dreamed, and smiled.

PEACH TREES

Do not hurry past this orchard too quickly
Saying: Yes, surely, that is a beautiful thing.
As though the moment of flaming were the
            purpose of this orchard
Accomplished now that your all-claiming eyes
            have seen it.
Remember that before these trees were ever planted,
A thin, small, unprotesting beast of burden
Dragged a curved plough through the reluctant earth,
With a man stooping behind in the hot sun to
            guide it.
Remember a wide ditch had to be dug here
            to coax the river
Up the dry, stubborn flanks of these hills, a
            long time barren,
And that a woman, ageless as the brown
            hills are ageless,
Hoed the difficult earth about the young roots planted,
And dreamed, before ever the slender branches
            had budded,
Of yellow fruit spread to the sun in her dooryard
            in autumn.

OLD HOUSE

This is the home of Epifanio Vigil and his
           wife Jesusita.
These walls were once earth at the edge of
           the earth-colored acequia.
They were fashioned into bricks by the hands
           of Epifanio,
And plastered by Jesusita.
See how white are these inner walls, how smooth
           the outer.
Time has gone over and over them so often,
Smoothing the roughness left by Jesusita's fingers
And the beam-corners carved by Epifanio.

Time and weather here are kind to houses.
After a space houses become one with the hillsides,
As calm, as everlasting, as unhurried.
The blue doorways and windows fade slowly
           into sky-color.
Even Epifanio Vigil and his wife Jesusita
Have become wind-carved and time-wrinkled
           and eternal.

BURROS

The brown hills,
The dust-colored burros,
Are secretly related.
There is nothing that seems as lazy under the sun;
Yet the burro carries bundles of cedar-wood
As big as himself and plods patiently
Anywhere you like, driven by ragged men
With quick smiles in brown, wind-wrinkled faces.

The hills
Hold centuries on their shoulders,
And march invisibly
Driven by old man Time.

Both hills and burros always laugh a little
At men who hurry.

RAIN

Rain is coming up the valley;
Rain is pouring out upon the mountains;
From a dark cloud heavy on the mountains
Rain is coming up the valley.

The river is a ribbon of brass unwound in silver.
Trees by the river turn silver under-leaves
To a lead sky.
Dust whirls through dry fields,
And tumbleweeds whirl dizzily down a roadway.

Rain is coming up the valley;
Rain rolling off the mountains;
Rain pouring through dry arroyos;
Rain in an angry wall of water
Higher than a man!

The young men are digging ditches,
And the old men build dams;
Ditches and dams to catch rain from the river.
The women set washtubs under rainspouts.
And hang blankets and petticoats on a wire fence
For the rain to wash.

The Rio Grande is tawny with Chama water;
Water from the red hills above Abiquiu;
From the clay hills beyond Chamita.
Rain glistens on lava cliffs by the Rio Grande
Like sweat on the smooth black flanks of
            a race-horse.
Like a swift horse rain is running through
            the valley!

Rain is a mist under leaves,
A silver frost,
A fragrance;
Fragrance of new-lain dust
Apple-scented, lavender-tinted, cool.
Rain is a shadow on a house-wall,
Or a gusty breath in an orchard,
Or a scud of color down a roadway.

Rain is passing like a song up the valley,
A light song, a love song, a thin song,
Played on one string of an old man's violin,
Accompanied by guitar.
Like a song rain is drifting up the valley!

ADMONITION

Perhaps we should have thought no more about it
Another time of year, but spring had spoken
In her first brave voice of apricot; in singing peach;
And then at last in a great, imploring chorus
Of fragrant apple. Orchards had awakened
On every valley-slanted hill; through every field
Wild plum ran riverward like a blown fire;
And over the walls of our ancient gardens
Pear trees lifted candle-white spires of bloom
Toward the sky. Our narrow, crooked streets
Were flinging before us around every curve
Some unexpected beauty. Petals rippled
Along the mad spring rush of the acequia;
And there were children entering the cathedral
With crisp white frocks, and blossoms in their hair.

How can they undrstand the beauty of our city
Who are not connoisseurs of loveliness?
For it is not a beauty of gay lights;
Nor of swift-moving crowds; nor quick young laughter;
Nor of shop-thronged streets; nor the sharp,
                    hard clink of money
Passing from fist to fist. Rather it is the beauty
Of an old, old woman in a black mantilla;

An old, old woman with unutterable wisdom
Behind her wordless reticence, who lights a candle
In token of prayer before a faded picture
Of the Madonna. Or it is humble beauty——
A flock of goats tumbling down a hill
At twilight; or a silent beauty
Of wine-dark shadows shed on purple hills.
Sometimes it is a silver pagan beauty
Of rain, cloud-feathered, running through the valley;
Of rain, a tall god running through the valley;
Sandalled with rivers. Sometimes it is the beauty
Of a saint's feast day; flowers before a shrine;
A new frock for the virgin——crimson silk
When she is carried over petalled streets
To San Rosario.

                    We cannot sell
The beauty of our city for a coin
Nor make a market-place for loveliness
Where loveliness is bred. We have awaked
Who should, perhaps, have thought no more about it
Another time of year. We have remembered
That in no other city could we find
Fruit trees by almost every blue-silled door;
Nor any other place where stars may shine
Serene, undimmed above the lighted streets.
Can we consent to have our trees give way
To flimsy houses, houses without trees?

Would men plant orchards for a summer's length
Or cherish them in time of drouth
With weary toil? Be warned, be warned
By all the exultant clamoring of spring!
Let not the bloom be ravaged lest the tree die
And no more fruit hang ripened from the bough!

ABIQUIU——THURSDAY IN HOLY WEEK

Is there any way I can be sure to remember
Abiquiu?
How the sun went down suddenly
Behind the hills, and the river darkened. Everything
Became sound only laid upon silence
          where had been lately
Bright houses and people moving past them,
          and dogs and children.

The moon was a long time coming up.
It came up slowly.
The hills grew tall and terrible before it. The long mesa
Behind Abiquiu was a huge blackness, growing blacker
On the slow silver sky.
The fields had been ploughed a little and we stumbled
          through them
Guiding our steps by grasping the budding willows
Beside the acequia. We didn't belong here.
This wasn't our world. We should never have come
          here at all.
We shivered and laid our lengths along the border
Of the field, a wall of low stone. The trail from
          the morada
Went past that wall. We heard something wailing
High in the hills. We waited.

A little beyond midnight they came out of the morada
And went past the wall, three of them, one singing;
One with the pito, the Penitente flute that is
                    more sorrowful
Than any sorrowful sound that was ever uttered
In music. The third man marched
With body bent a little forward. At the end
                    of each line of singing
He brought the woven whip across his shoulders
With a lashing sound, rhythmical, like an accent;
A sound that was dull and harsh, as though already
Blood softened the lean back. A lantern flickered
In the hand of the singer. Its swinging shadow
Was swallowed soon in darkness.

I, under the cold stars, there in the cold night, watching
This greatest of remembered tragedies enacted
By men who as soon as Easter was over
Would go back to their ordinary way of living——
To the fields they must finish plowing and sowing;
To the sheep that would be lambing soon in the canyons;
To the ditches that must be cleared to flood
                    the orchards,
Each man when his turn came, from the mother
                    acequia——
Men whose brown, wind-lined faces I had often
                    seen passing
In wagons loaded with wood brought down
                    from the mesas

Behind Abiquiu, or driving burros
Slowly, as if in some other country, along the highway.
I, crouched there against the cold stone, prone
            on the cold earth, listening;
Thought: There is something they know, these men,
            that we have forgotten;
They remember, here in these mountains, here
            at Abiquiu on this spring night,
On this unforgettable Thursday before Easter,
That to imitate simply, unaware even of any
            special meaning
A great and tragic action, is to be lifted by it
For a moment out of commonplace living
            toward greatness.

A MIRACLE OF SANTUARIO

From Santa Cruz to Chimayo
Is not so long as long miles go.
From Chimayo to Truchas town
The road goes up, the hills are brown,
And there the Truchas mountains rise
A sharp blue step into the skies.

Juan Torres rode from Truchas town
Before the sun looked to the south.
The mountains leaned a weary weight;
The devil's thirst was in his mouth.
Juan Torres stopped at Chimayo.
He saw the church doors opened wide;
The warm, sweet shadows tempted him;
He mounted down and stepped inside.
He left the cold breath of the sky;
He left the hard touch of the hill;
He knelt down like a man of faith,
But the devil's thirst was on him still.
He could not pray. Dios! he cried,
I have no money to buy drink
In Santa Cruz this eventide.

Nothing happened in the little church.
Mary Virgin looked calmly down on the faded blossoms
And the white, windless candles before her,
And there was a stillness, a moving stillness
Everywhere, as under a wing-spread shadow.

> Juan Torres got up from his knees;
> Juan Torres looked to left and right;
> He was alone, and on the wall
> A saint shone under candle-light——
> San José carved in fading wood,
> With stiff, straight robe, with still, sad face,
> And on his arm the holy child
> Smiling in ancient, painted grace.
> Juan Torres' heart leapt like a thought;
> He saw no watcher thereabout;
> He lifted Joseph from the wall
> And blew the wavering candle out.

The new-leaved trees were motionless against the sky,
The two great trees that had seen many come and go
Over the worn threshold of the sanctuary.
They did not bend now to accuse Juan Torres.

> He lashed his horse from Chimayo;
> He rode like one whom death pursues;
> And when the stars marched up the sky
> He came at last to Santa Cruz.
> His young wife met him at the door;
> Her eyes were dark and deep with fear.

He would not let her speak at all
But cried: Luz, see what I have here!
San José carved in ancient wood.
The rich Americans will pay
A lot of money for these things
At any store in Santa Fé.
Tomorrow I can sell him quick.
Tonight I go to ask a loan,
And buy a gallon of good stuff
From Señor Pedro Gabaldon.

Juan Torres swaggered out into the cold, black night.
His young wife, Luz, stood like a stricken thing,
Then crossed herself and went down on her knees
Before the San José carelessly laid on the table.
Outside the stars went over in the wide sky
And each one seemed to halt accusingly
One moment over the little house of Juan Torres.
The hills drew themselves up against the night
Like a marching army.

Luz Torres knelt and cried to God,
Luz Torres' heart was white and pure,
Though she had stood more
        from dark-souled Juan
Than any woman should endure.
Three children she had borne to him
That had not lived to touch her breast.

And in her womb the fourth lay now
That suddenly moved and would not rest,
That suddenly leapt against her heart.
And Luz bowed down in heavy pain
Knowing it felt its father's sin
And she must bear a corpse again.
Santa Maria! she cried aloud,
This sin is not mine, but I must pay.
I must do penance. I must atone.
Dios! Maria! Show me the way.

The stars came closer and stopped. The hills opened.
The hills opened and showed Luz the wall of a chapel,
With a niche on the wall, empty, and a candle unlighted,
And a road winding a long way, over rivers.

Juan Torres stumbled in at the doorway,
          hot-mouthed, heavy-breathed.
He laughed and pawed at Luz kneeling, her
          head turned downward.
That's right, he said. Say your prayers to the old man.
Tomorrow he will bring us a lot of money,
More than he ever did for us hanging
          on the wall at Santuario.
And he lurched to the cot in the corner and
          fell heavily on it.
Luz shuddered. Her narrow face was wan
          in the lamplight.
There was a light behind it like the light in a painting

Of a saint's head. She brought her black mantilla
Out of a corner by the chimney and drew it over her
So that she looked more than ever
                    like a frightened Mary
Painted on an old tabla. With one look at Juan
She took the image and hid it beneath her mantilla.
She went out into the night with it as though
                    she were holding an infant.

            From Santa Cruz to Chimayo
            Is not so long as long miles go.
            Against the faint arch of the sky
            The dark hills are heaped mountain high;
            Beyond the hills the mountains stand.
            A river runs through the wide sand,
            And there are houses, dim and white,
            Unlighted in the cold, late night.

No one saw Luz Torres running in the night;
No one saw Luz Torres with a burden in her body,
                    a burden in her arms
Becoming heavier, heavy as the sin on the
                    soul of Juan Torres
Who had stolen the saint from Santuario for money.
No one saw, as she marched, the hills reach
                    higher and higher
And shed the light from their shoulders and
                    burn with glory
Like the evening radiance that names them
                    Sangre de Cristo.

page 36

No one saw the waiting trees in the orchards
Flame into blossom as though a torch had
                    touched them.
No one saw Luz Torres sink under her burden
By a row of little Penitente crosses. No one
                    heard the stars singing,
Nor the cries of a woman in travail, nor an
                    infant wailing.
The image Luz Torres dropped in her anguish
                    by the road side
Was one moment a wooden San José
                    stern-faced, dust-colored;
The next, tall as a man who stooped a moment.
Who was there to see when he rose he carried
                    two infants
And supported a woman with a face like Mary's
Along the dusty road to Chimayo?

> Juan Torres woke from weighted sleep.
> The sun was tall in the day's sky,
> And in his startled, lingering dream
> He thought he heard a child's thin cry.
> He lay like one who tries to think
> Of something that must soon be done
> And could not think. Then someone called
> And said: Your Luz has borne a son!
> He rose and gazed on her thin face.
> The day, the night had passed away.
> He stooped to take her in his arms
> As though it were their marriage day.

His mind held not one sinful thought.
His soul was like a child's and white.
He cried to Luz: Why, look, the trees
Have blossomed early, in one night!

II

FIVE YEARS OLD

There was a field, I know, all warm with sun,
Purple with asters blown through golden grass;
And a stone wall where huckleberries grew,
Broken in places so a child could pass.
Beyond the wall the field became a hill
That slyly steepened till a child must run,
Arms flung against the wind, to finally spill
With small brown feet and buttons half undone
Into the laughing ripples of the lake;
There to stand still as still and feel the sand
Crinkle between bare toes, or wade knee-deep
Along the shore; to startle small green frogs
And little lazy turtles fast asleep;

Or to run hand in hand with wind again,
Happily truant, up an ancient lane
Where lilacs grew in weirdly twisted trees
Fragrant with flowers and frightening with bees;
To break great armfuls off, all warmly sweet,
Then flee pursuing bees on startled feet;
And mother-wanting now and all afraid
Willingly seek the nursery's tranquil shade.

There might be bread and milk in a deep bowl,
The silver mug, and the short, stubby spoon
She loved the best. But sometimes they would scold
The child for running from her nap at noon
And send her supperless away instead.
Then she would cry awhile in the bright room,
Little and tired, all crumpled in the bed
Until the shadows vanished in the gloom
And whippoorwills and owls commenced to call;
Before her mother tiptoed softly near
She'd be asleep, forgetful of it all.

A DOWER FOR MY DAUGHTER

If I can give you these things
I shall be content
And count the days of motherhood
Well enough spent:

Eyes that find beauty in
Shadows on the wall,
And candle-light at tea-time
And pear trees tall;
Ears that welcome soft rain
Whispering at night,
And wind on the mountain
And birds at first light;

A heart that can find comfort
In walking alone
On a tree-grown hillside
Till grief has flown;
Or that can stand in trouble
As trees in rain
Lovelier than ever when
The light comes again.

Silver I have not,
Nor a purse of gold,
To buy you soft raiment
And jewels to hold.
But the beauty your heart knows
And your eyes can see
Will never cost a penny;
It is always free.

Nothing more of motherhood
Shall I demand
Than to give you ears to hear
And heart to understand.

IF I HAD A YOUNG SON

If I had a young son
I would have him merry
And full of laughter
And bright as a berry.
I'd like it if he'd
Believe in dragons
And go out to kill them
In small, red wagons.
It would be nicest
If he'd not doubt
Brownies drank milk
That he set out.
And I'd think it best
To have him play
Out in the woods
Alone all day;
For trees are secret
And birds are shy,
And never talk
With grown-ups by.

Then when he gets bigger
Perhaps he'll be
Eager for knowing
The land and sea.
I never will keep him
By my side
But give him a strong horse
And let him ride
As far as he wants to,
As far as he can,
And all round the world when
He is a man!

FOR A BIRTHNIGHT

Your birth came on a night of stars.
A windless sliver of a moon
Lost on the ebb-tide of the day
Drifted beyond the mountains soon.

And when they laid you in my arms
The pine trees were like silent spars
Against the pale edge of the sky,
Against the gleam of stars.

And so I thought what fairy child,
What changeling elf has come to me
That trees and stars stand still to watch
And all the winds are hushed to see?

TO A VERY LITTLE BOY

You are my dear love.
I would like you to be altogether mine.
I would like us to live in the world all by ourselves
So that I could offer you the stars
            (as if they belonged to no other)
And no one but you and I could make footprints
            in the snow.

NOT QUITE THREE

How can I make a picture of you
To keep for always and always
Just as you are at this moment?

Brown eyes like a small, friendly puppy;
Brown curls you haven't learned to be ashamed of,
Curls to tangle wind in; a wise forehead;
Lips as bright as barberry, as gay as barberry;
And at the corner of your mouth one dimple
That runs in and out all day like an elf
Playing pranks and laying snares of laughter;
A firm body, half baby-curves, half boy-sturdiness,
And full of bubbling life that makes you skip
Sometimes, and hop, and move in sudden jumps
Like a young goat.

Sometimes I think
You've always been part faun, or have the power
To change to one. I'm sure I've seen
Your ears go pointed under the spilled curls,
And I've heard hoofbeats very small and sharp
As though a young faun danced.

Perhaps someday
I'll hear myself, if I am ever asked,
Saying I planted a nut once underneath a fern
And then found you, wrapped in a woodbine leaf!

SONG FOR HANGING OUT CLOTHES

I pin them quickly to the line,
All dripping in a row,
As white and sweet as any sails
To tempt the winds that blow.

As white as if I'd caught the clouds
That hurry through the sky
And wrung the rain all out of them,
And hung them up to dry!

BONDAGE

I am held back from flight by such small things:
A flannel shirt unfolded on a chair
Needs a patch badly. Who am I to care,
Who have been born for flight and sky-spread wings?
And yet I'll stay and mend it; run new strings
Into the baby's bib; and shine the pair
Of copper candle-sticks, and while I'm there
Rub up the kettle till it almost sings.
As long as there are plates to wash and dry
Or towels to hem or bowls for mixing cake
Or cookies, or a petticoat to make
I'll have to stay. I cannot run away.
And so I'll sing and mend a toy and sigh
And make believe I'll go another day.

ESCAPE

She hid herself in a bird
That clung to a wire,
In a bird with tempestuous wings
And a throat of fire.

She hid herself in a cloud,
And she fell as rain
Musically on the grass
In a leaf-lit lane.

Oh, she was so grave and silent,
So shy of a word,
That no one guessed she went swinging
On the wire in a bird.

None of us even missed her
Until we learned
She had fled in a leaf blown skyward
And never returned.

DO NOT FEEL SURE

Do not feel sure that she will be long contented
In this house you have built for her.
She will love it all for a while. She will love to stir
Softly out in her kitchen all alone,
Placing her thin blue cups along the shelves
Spread with white paper;
Pinning a row of dripping towels, sky-blown
Like checkered sails to a frosty, silver wire;
Or cutting with one quick, eager turn of wrist
Into a bright gold orange.
You'll not believe that she can ever tire
Of resting tranquilly in your embrace,
Turning her sun-flushed face
Up to your cooler one to have it kissed,
Or seeking the warm, sure shelter of your hand
For her firm-fingered one.
But I know she was not meant for times like these.
She was made to dwell
Upon a stern dark edge of wilderness,
To watch men hew the barrier line of trees
And lay them log on log; with her own hands
To chink the wall that kept the wind outside.
She would have borne ten children sturdily,

Strong, brown-limbed boys and tall, wind-ripened girls.
Eager for bearing as a fertile tree,
She would not be appeased by mothering
One child or two as women are today.
She was not meant to buy life ready-made
But to do battle for it.
Someday she'll go
Swift as a loosened fox across the snow
And you'll not see her anymore.
How do I know?
Well, I've known wild things bred a hundred years
Till they forget the look of winter moons,
Silver of frost splintered on autumn grass,
The click of a pointed hoof, the cry of loons;
Till they forget the quiet, fear-white land,
The sharp-ribbed, silent hunger stalking it,
And what it is for parent beasts to stand
With strong, fierce pride between the seeking death
And their blind, whimpering young.
She is like that!
But the first, familiar shadow will waken her,
Or the first faint flicker of a star-sent cry
Or an old, old hunger making remembered stir
Will call her back more than a hundred years.
For all your tears
She will not once look back. If you are wise
You will not often let her be alone
To listen to the wind or watch the skies.
You will not let her bear one child for you

Lest in her ecstasy and in her pain
She should awaken to her hungry need
Of mothering ten.
When once she knows, she will not rest again
Or turn to you or pay you any heed.
She will make flight too swift for you to follow
Like a fear-fleet deer, or a wild, wind-driven swallow.

CHANGELING

She was not quite mortal
And not quite fay
Though she sometimes laughed
In a human way;
Though she sometimes stood
As quiet as a tree
And shone when the rain fell
Silverly.

A thing possessed
The women thought her,
And dared to say
She was no man's daughter.

For the way she danced
Was beyond belief,
Like a small winged bird
Or a crisp, gold leaf;
And the way she talked
Was a thing worth knowing,
Like the wind on water
Or a white tree blowing.

Men have gone mad who
Tried to hold her,
For she lay like a wind
Against their shoulder;
As cool as a shadow,
As chaste as air
She'd lie in a man's arms
And never care.
She would much rather
Sleep in a tree
Than under a sheet
Companionably!

But none of us knew
The things she said
Except her mother
And the lad she wed:

That if water called her,
Or a still sky,
Her thoughts would leave her,
Her thoughts would fly

Down to the water
Or through the air;
She would feel stars tangled
In her hair.
Or silver fishes

Would seem to glide
With a queer flicker
Against her side.

Someday she might not
Get back at all,
She thought, if they should
Forget to call.
He must not leave her,
She said, too long
To hear the wind
Or the water's song.

And then this happened,
A queer, sad thing;
We could not find them
One day in spring.
We looked in the woods
And on the hill;
We called and called
But the trees were still.

It was almost twilight
Before we found
Them beside the water.
He was drowned,
And her image under
The leaf-spun moon

Was like last year's nest
Or an old cocoon.
Like an empty dress
She was sitting there
Without a thought in her
Anywhere.

Her mother said:
It's a queer, sad thing,
But I bore her under
A tree in spring.
You have said true
She is no man's daughter
Who was born in April
By running water.

Whatever man
May have tried to hold her
Found her wind
Against his shoulder.
And the man who weds child
Of the wind and rain
Will lose her always
To them again.

SHADOW-MADNESS

They say her house is shadow-haunted now
Who while she lived loved shadows more than life.
She sought them everywhere. A saffron bough
Of autumn leaves was lovelier to her
If imaged upward from a pool of rain——
Reflections lie so softly with no stir
On wind-neglected water!

                    In her room
She tempted shadows with smooth surfaces,
Loving the way the shapes of common things
Bent into strangeness. Even orchard bloom
Was only sweet when on her wall the moon
Painted the silver image.

                    Every day
She polished carefully each knife and spoon
To see them shine; rubbed rainbows once again
Into each glass; then finished washing up
By blowing bubbles through her finger-tips.
The curving image of each star-gold cup
Hung soap-imprisoned for bewitching her.

She married one in whom she seemed to see
Her love reflected. She had thought to show
The magic of her shadow-world to him,
But he was bound fast to reality.
He liked a thing for its essential form,
Not the distorted image that it cast;
And so she slipped away from him at last.
He held her body but her thoughts became
Fleeting as images of blowing leaves
Wind-blurred on water. He was not to blame
Who could not grasp intangibility,
For she had been created shadow-mad
And vanished like the shadow with the flame.

TO CERTAIN ONES
WHO DO NOT UNDERSTAND

All of her days go similarly by,
Smoothly as water in a meadow stream,
Softly as silken clouds in a still sky,
Silent as a slow, star-awakened dream.
But do not pity her who yet has known
No sharp-edged joy, no bitter-pointed pain;
Who has not met grief in the night, alone;
Who with no piercing love has ever lain.

She lives more poignantly than you can guess
Who are too dull to know the ecstasies,
With sun-touched hills, of a long, slow caress
Of moving light on wind-hushed grass and trees;
Who have not felt swept by the wings of birds;
Nor pricked by firs along a mountain-side;
Nor stung by stars like little, burning words;
Nor stricken like sky at storm's approaching stride.

She becomes part of earth with every spring
And bears earth's blossoming as if her own,
Knowing a birth-pain for each lovely thing,
For ice-freed lakes, for orchards apple-blown.
The joy of hills is hers, serene and high;
Hers is each pool of quiet, rain-touched grief;
And when her autumn comes, and she must die,
She will go radiantly like a sky-tossed leaf!

BRIDAL

The slow wind rippled moonlight on the floor
While she lay wakeful. Rustling feet soft-furred
Spread rings of sound in the grass like water-blurred
Shadows of splashing leaves. Beyond the door
Fell a flood of silver light that seemed to pour
In showers from all the trees. Far off she heard
The questioning call of a star-awakened bird
And thought she could not lie there any more
Against his arm. She would have slipped from bed
And run, moon-white, far up the fragrant lane
Of heavy-flowering trees. She would have stood
Star-cooled upon the hill above the wood.
But suddenly he stirred and woke again
And sleepily stretched his arm beneath her head.

HITHERTO

Hitherto I have written
That only which I saw with my eyes,
Which my ears heard, which my mouth could taste.
For the stirring of my blood,
That immense roaring of oceans when I touched
                your hand,
I have not any words.

CEREMONIAL

Once in every year
Let us go up into this high mountain
Where the gods live, where beauty walks, hungry
              for habitation.
Let us incarnate the gods here in these bodies
Where the grass lies in the wind against the mountain
Under the dwarfed trees, under the singing-leaved
              aspens,
Close on the wide-ringed shadows of the spruce trees.

Here on this mountain at the time when earth is most
              beautiful
Let us leave off all our disguises, all our garments
              stained with the sweat of the ascending.
Let us love each other as though we were gods become
              human for a moment.
It will not be my breast that feels your weight then,
              but the breast of mouhtain.
It will be a spear of fire from that cloud that shall
              have pierced me.

EVERGREEN

Dear, I have watched the wind upon the hill
Running to take the birch trees with caress;
And I have watched the maple leaves athrill
Desirous of his touch. With blowing dress
White aspens run,—— they really almost run,
Eager as girls to take their lover's kiss.
Sometimes I wonder, would you have me be
Birch-like, or maple-like, show eager bliss
Like aspens when they're kissed? Oh not for me
Their wild, ecstatic ways. I am a fir
Meeting the wind with vast tranquillity.
I seem to take your love with little stir;
But——autumn strips a birch tree of its song,
While firs are evergreen the whole year long!

AFTER LOOKING INTO A GENEALOGY

Time is not, when I remember you, my grandmothers.
Your bones, your flesh have gone into the dust;
From granite stones the wind has wiped your names.
The years have trod your graves flat with the earth,
You who were beautiful, you who died still young
In childbirth, you who saw
Ninety and more full years before you passed,
Whose husbands died at sea, whose husbands died
In the stern winters of a wilderness.

Time is not, when I remember you, my grandmothers.
Mercy and Lydia and Abigail,
Ruth and Mehitable; sea-captains' wives,
Daughters of soldiers, mothers of men of God;
Statira, Betsey, Patience, Margery,
Remember, whose other name the gravestones have
                forgotten.

Out of old books these names, from moldering stones,
All that is left of you, my grandmothers!
                All but the blood
That makes me one with you. The blood that cried
Like a wanderer returned when I first saw——

page 68

I, the desert-born, this offspring
            of New England growing
Among New Mexico mountains—— when I first saw
The dogwood blossoming in Connecticut woods,
The meadows sprinkled with a rain of daisies,
The apple-orchard set in low, green hills.

I know now why in my dreams I had seen those hills
            and had remembered
The covered bridges over Vermont rivers,
And why, whenever I came upon a clearing
            in mountain country
I thought: One could build a house here.
That slope would make a pasture. An orchard
            would be fruitful
In a few years, and the apples fragrant.
The butter I'd churn would be cool and sweetened
In a stone house over this mountain-spewed
            thread of water.

When I was a little girl
My mother kept the milk in a house
            built half underground
With shelves around the walls. There the warm milk
            yellowed
With heavy cream in rows of shallow pans. Something
            familiar,
Something not remembered first stirred in me
When I crept down to watch her.

But most of all, my grandmothers, your blood leaps
                    in me
(Obliterating time, making of me one person with my
                    forebears,
One person who has lived since life crawled up
                    from the waters
And became man, who will not die
Till the last woman of this race is barren)
Most of all, my blood stirs with your voices
When the winds of winter thunder like ocean water
And the white snow whirls down in utter darkness.

Then I remember, or it seems as if I remembered,
The earliest winter, and the fierce grey water
Heaped between us and England (that grey water
Cradling more than one of my grandfathers)
The desperate stand we made against that winter,
The bitter battle.

We were sturdy-limbed, the daughters of that winter.
We had inherited strength that must be tried.
                    We could not
Live and grow old, unrestless, in security,
And so we went off, shoulder to shoulder with our men,
                    and singing,
Into the farther wilderness.

In these days, my grandmothers, the weak live easily.
The weak crowd out the strong like weeds
          in an untilled garden.
Where can we go, we in whom your blood sings?——
The eager blood of our forefathers, of our foremothers,
          who marched chin forward
And always toward the horizon?

I HAVE LOOKED AT THE EARTH

And you said: I am afraid to have you fly.
Had you forgotten that afternoon on Point Lobos
When, because the tide of centuries that had swept over
    those rocks somehow washed over us with the sound
    of unceasing water, and because there was so much
    life there in the color of tree-shadowed sky and voices
    invisible and not human,
We said that the more we could be aware of the world,
    of the color and sound of it, of its taste in our mouths
    and the feel of it under our fingers,
The more we could perhaps remember and recognize and
    regain of its beauty
After death had stripped us of our familiar tools for seeing
    and listening and touching?
We thought, for the space of an afternoon, with the
    thought of rocks. The deep heart of the earth,
    muffled and unhurried, sounded through us. We al-
    most took root there, forgetting we were human and
    mortal, becoming earth there at the sea's edge.

When we are dead we know this one thing will become
    of us:
We will go into the ground; our bodies will surely
    crumble and feed tree-roots, or blow as dust on the

wind or be rain-washed at last into ocean.
Is it this you fear for me, bidding me not fly, bidding
me go carefully and save this body?

If there were any more danger in flying than always in
living, when death hangs ever invisible above our
heads, and we never know at what instant the
thread will be cut that holds it,
Would it be so dreadful to drop, in an interval of ecstasy,
in a fear-escaping second, out of this human exist-
ence, to go back to earth and be one in the constel-
lations, to give birth to mountains, to be intimate
with the tide and the rain and the seasons?

I have known these moments of unlimited happiness:
That afternoon on Point Lobos that was like going home
out of an alien country;
A moment on Tsacoma Mountain where the tides of the
air are shattered like waves and become clouds, and
go down as rain on the sea-forgotten valley;
And that moment of flying over the Mojave. The pain
of death at that moment would not have been greater
than my heart bore at beholding earth naked and
virgin with the shadow of twilight above her like
a lover.
Each of these moments was like a sudden dying, a brief
escape from the body, an instant of being the beauty
which, living, we only taste a little.
Oh never fear death for me for I have looked at the
earth and loved it. I have been part of earth's beauty
in moments beyond the edge of living.

Two hundred fifty copies of
FORETASTE
have been handset in Caslon Old Style
printed and bound by
The Rydal Press

www.ingramcontent.com/pod-product-compliance
Lightning Source LLC
Chambersburg PA
CBHW022012080426
42733CB00007B/577